BLACK & BOLD

I'M NOT A NURSE

JESSICA BAILEY

This first edition published in 2022.
Copyright © Jessica Bailey.

All rights reserved. No part of this book may be reproduced or transmitted by any means, electronic or mechanical, including photocopying, recording, or by any information storage and retrieval system, without prior permission in writing from the publisher. The Australian *Copyright Act* 1968 (the Act) allows a maximum of one chapter or 10 per cent of this book, whichever is the greater, to be photocopied by any educational institution for its educational purposes, provided that the educational institution (or body that administers it) has given a remuneration notice to the Copyright Agency (Australia) under the Act.

>Black & BOLD
>Australia
>hello@blackandbold.au
>blackandbold.au

Cataloguing-in-publication details are available from the National Library of Australia at www.trove.nla.gov.au.

>ISBN 978-0-6456-069-0-4

Cover by David Schembri Studios – davidschembristudios.com – dschembristudios@gmail.com.
Typeset in Jost and Baskerville Old Face.
Printed and bound in Australia by IngramSpark.

Contents

Preface

Chapter 1: *Ejechi*	01
Chapter 2: Passion	07
Chapter 3: Hollywood	17
Chapter 4: Now What?	23
Chapter 5: Join Them	31
Chapter 6: No Shortcut	37
Chapter 7: Dilemma	43
Chapter 8: White Faces	49
Chapter 9: Run!	53
Chapter 10: Not a Nurse	61
Chapter 11: Home	73
Chapter 12: Cumar	77
Chapter 13: Not So Scary	83
Chapter 14: When it Rains	91

Afterword   101

Preface

During my first few years in Australia, I felt like I was in a nightmare, struggling to create and follow my own path. My journey of self-discovery left me yearning to cement my own creative identity. I started to imagine this journey as a story in itself, and it was out of this process that an original project was created, which was first written as a screenplay entitled *I'm Not a Nurse*. It tells the story of a young African woman who has a passion for filmmaking, but the colour of her skin is a barrier which she must fight to overcome if she is to achieve her dream.

Before I came to Australia, I did not understand that I would get caught up in an unwritten code which would decide for me where I would belong. This decision would be based on my culture and the colour of my skin, without asking about the skills, knowledge, special talents, international connections and other benefits which I brought with me.

Once I realised what was happening, I decided to challenge the traditional migrant career path of nursing or some other service industry profession. I fought my way through the opposition and over the hurdles; I survived, and I found my voice, which helped me to represent myself and contribute positively to Australia. My question since then has been: what about the others? What about the ones who weren't as brave, or privileged enough to be able to challenge this code? What happens to them? What happens to their voice? What happens to their talents? How can they better contribute to Australia while they're still being caught in the trap of this unwritten code?

When I began to share my story in Australia, what I did not know is that I was sharing the stories of many migrants. At one point, I paused and realised that while our stories are similar, I challenged this norm and overcame it. But this code has swallowed and suppressed too much talent and too many leaders in Australia because they were not given sufficient chance to demonstrate how they could best contribute and further develop this country.

I know that many migrants of colour are still caught in this trap. I know that there will be many more migrants who come and will face these challenges. I am sharing my story to say that there has been enough of this unwritten code. I want to inspire others who are like me so that they get to find their voice and use it effectively to contribute to a greater Australia.

Jessica Bailey
September 2022

Chapter 1: *Ejechi*

When I was little, my mother would warn everyone – even strangers – to be wary about my stories. 'The only truth Ifelunwa tells is "good morning" – but even then, check that it is actually a good morning.' My mother uses the name she chose for me, which means *golden child*. Though she would make these comments in whispers to start with, they would grow louder. 'No one makes up stories in my family. You picked it up from your Aunty Cele. You're exactly like her.'

Thanks to my mother, people learned to fasten their seat belts when I was talking. But it upset me to know that people wouldn't take my stories seriously. The reason we get emotional with movies is because we take them as if the characters and the stories are real. And to me, the seasoning that I added to the stories was necessary. 'The car almost hit the girl,' would not get the same reaction as if I were to say, 'The car hit the girl and it ground her to pieces, creating a pool of blood that formed an entire river!'

Since my mother started giving away my secret, the worst part is that, when I tell stories that really happened, my siblings choke on their laughter whenever I start, unable to wait for me to finish before running outside, ready to burst. I get annoyed by it, even though I don't blame my mother.

My mother is a poor widow, and in this village, words did not just grow legs, they grew arms and wings and they travelled faster than anything. If the wrong words eventually landed on the wrong ears, my whole family would be in trouble and would pay dearly. Through all the years that my lies and storytelling lasted, there was not a day that went by that my poor mother did not wish I was different. I baffled everyone by spinning a tiny event into a story, turning words – just words – into a bomb blast that could damage an entire village.

It was safe for my mother to blame this character flaw on my father's side – she was probably right. Aunty Cele is a beautiful liar. She is known for her made-up stories, and if there were an award for such talent, my aunty would be a frontrunner. Apply a lie detector and you would still not find them, she is that good. If anyone trusted her, my uncle's wife would say, 'Don't act on Cele's words,' and chuckle.

But Cele's blood flowed in my veins, too.

By the time I was in junior high, my brother and I were living with my uncle and his family in their two-bedroom apartment in Obiaruku, Nigeria.

I lost my dad when I was eleven years old. After that, we lost our home to my dad's family members, who accused my mum of destroying him. It's a typical story that goes with deaths in Nigeria; someone must be held responsible. His family left us out in the cold and they were not sorry. We relocated to my mum's village, but we were pushed out. My maternal grandmother chased us before we could walk into her house because she was still upset with my mother for disobeying her by marrying my father.

When my mother found out she was pregnant with me, she was told to get rid of me or lose her job. She chose to keep me and that became life for her - a struggling young woman with no job and no husband. My father was at university in Nsukwa, completing his degree on a scholarship.

I could never confidently apply for scholarships like he did – I couldn't see myself as being qualified to even sit an exam for one. My frightened mind always told me that scholarships are for the intelligent. Sometimes I would question my thinking about who I considered 'intelligent', because I could objectively analyze the situation: in a class of 50 students in high school, I would be at the top. I maintained my status as a prefect or assistant prefect – which was a privilege given to the best students – throughout secondary school. I only missed out on being a Senior Prefect.

By the time I got to my final year in secondary school, the teenager in me had started to kick in. I wanted so badly to have a taste of what it meant to be a bad student, because it meant getting more attention. There were always wide eyes on those students who got called out to the assembly ground every morning on bad behaviour: for leaving school during school hours, for taking to the bush, for abusing school uniforms, and smoking. Tucking in my shirt and wearing socks were no longer a thing. I developed an 'I don't care' attitude, leaving school during school hours and returning whenever I pleased. I started to explore all of it—got myself a boyfriend too, something I wouldn't have done in earlier years. I tasted not just what the bad students tasted, but also what my parents had been tasting and for me, that made me their equal.

As I did all of this, the teachers were watching. I noticed, but my small-minded brain did not take stock of the consequences.

I was spoiled. I had been born with a critical health condition which led to everyone – especially my mum – sacrificing so much. I was the kind of child that people called *ejechi*, meaning 'to die and return' in Ukwuani. I used to faint at least five times every week—certainly not your everyday child, or the child one would hope for. But my mother made sure I always received all of her love.

I had always thought that problems – no matter how small – are for adults to solve. Even when I become an adult, I still don't see myself as an adult. Luckily for me, I've always had bigger adults around me, and my mum is the biggest one. I looked up to her, always, to chase even the smallest mosquitoes away before I could detect their presence. My mother had never failed at this, and this only increased my confidence that I am right.

This effect followed me even as I grew older and met other people in other places. Strangers that didn't know my story would want to do things for me that I should be doing for myself. I stayed firm in the knowledge that there was someone else to solve the problem. I would approach situations like a toddler because everything had always been given to me.

We had not been living with my uncle and his family for very long before I began telling my stories to them. They would take everything I said very seriously. I can still remember the shocked face of my uncle's wife when I told her that I had escaped a massacre. Guerilla soldiers were shooting helter-skelter with their AK-47s, chasing us on the way home from school. I had survived death by an inch.

She was in awe that I had been so lucky. Not very many people who encountered an automatic assault rifle stayed alive. 'Ifelunwa, come and share to Mummy Digbue how you survived death,' my uncle's wife exclaimed. Mummy Digbue is our landlord's wife. 'They only missed Ifelunwa by a step.'

I take the space with confidence. The stage is mine, and my mission is to hold everyone hostage.

Every single day, I practice mimicking news presenters on TV. I want to read and sound exactly like them. I would take one quick glance at the newspaper or textbook in my hand, then look at my audience as I read the lines, back and forth, on and on. There is something about the people living inside the box in the corner of our living room. The sophisticated presenters all sound so put-together when they speak with an English accent.

I can do it for movies too. Others would watch films for entertainment while I watch to learn about acting. The actors are attractive, smart, and versatile. I watch Nollywood movies over and over, rehearsing every line of dialogue and every character in front of the mirror, their relationships with one another and their emotions… There is nothing I want more. I was made to do the same and my whole being has always known it. It is only a matter of biding my time until I become the TV star I was born to be.

I practice until I master it enough to present it to my secondary schoolmates. They form a circle around me under a mango tree near our assembly ground, listening to my story with their eyes wide and their jaws dropped.

'You narrate so well,' one of them would compliment.

'You make it feel as though we're watching it,' another would applaud.

Comments like theirs only validate what I already know: I am a storyteller.

This is why my mother worried, and why she used to warn strangers about me – but my uncle and his family learn the hard way. And when they finally understand that I am just like Aunty Cele, the shit hits the fan and I am chased out of the house.

Life comes with challenges and challenges are meant to be responded to. However, when it comes to challenges, I only know one thing: *run*.

One hot afternoon, when I took a plank of wood with a nail through it and bashed Emmanuel's head until he bled, I ran. When I accidentally hit a little girl with my bicycle on my way to school, I ran. When that 4-year-old kid threw himself into my motorbike and collapsed, I ran.

It's what I do.

Chapter 2: Passion

'Why are we not on your TV?' Lucas is looking at me, asking as if he's only noticing this for the first time. I am shocked. Black African people are not on his screen – the one that streams in English every night and day while he sips on red wine and crunches on Barbecue Shapes. My anger boils. How could he be oblivious to the fact that the movies and songs and ads that run 24 hours per day on his services – the ones that represent his world – do not have my people? I want to scream at him that his TV does not show people who look like the woman seated beside him – the woman he has travelled thousands of miles with to have as a wife. How could he not be aware of this?

Back in Nigeria, we only know about the existence of the White people through television. We have cable TV networks which feed us White content. This is how we learned that we are not the only people on the planet. As a kid, I wondered where White people lived and what they look like in real life. Now, here I am in a White land, and the White man beside me does not recognise me as Black African – he seems to pretend that my home and my people do not exist!

Lucas soon learns. My curiosity about the lack of people who look like me on TV isn't for the fun of it. This is my dream, my passion.

I hopped on the marriage boat with Lucas because he's kind. When he asked me to marry him, it seemed no different to someone asking me to go for a walk – I was young and innocent and oblivious. Lucas asked me to marry him the same way he had asked me to go with him to Australia, and my response was the same.

'Come with me to Australia?'

'Okay. Where is Australia?' I giggled as I snacked on the foreign Mars Bar chocolate that he had brought me. I was bold, confident, and too young to make deeper meaning of the life that surrounded me, but smart enough to know that things would be better abroad. This seemed like an opportunity. Africa, the land that witnessed my first cry, had shown no compassion to dreams and its dreamers wish for nothing more than to soar far, far, away.

I boarded a plane with him. Two days after that, we landed in Australia – a country I had barely heard of beforehand. Lucas wanted me to meet his family: his mum, two gorgeous children, dad, and sister. Australia looked great: the trees, the peaceful ocean, the breathtaking blue sky and the bright stars that sit perfectly on it at night, the smooth roads and the immaculate streetlights. The smiley faces of strangers and the manicured lawns all looked charming and unreal. It never seemed like there was going to be any sacrifice.

Lucas loves me. A lot. And so does his family, who wholeheartedly accepted me, even before they met me. But I have a dream, and I want to pursue it. I will not be tied down and watch it slip from my fingers, even for a perfect country and a perfect marriage.

The question is: how far can I go with this? How much am I willing to sacrifice to remain in Australia? I have crossed many borders to get here. I have travelled over many seas, flown in many planes. When my mother asks me about the distance to Australia, the best way that I can describe it is to say that I am living in another world.

The fact that Australia doesn't allow people like me a space to practice my passion makes it feel like a threat to me, and as always, I feel the need to run before more trouble unfolds.

I grow angry in Australia. I live in what we call *a mansion* – six bedrooms and three large living rooms – and I should be happy, but I am not. I have a husband that loves me dearly and a family in-law who loves me equally and I should be happy, but I am not.

I become oblivious to all of the beauties that exist in Australia. I have my God-given long legs and charming smile and irresistible voice and I am to shove them all away, under a blanket.

On top of that, I think I am being starved. I am swallowing tasteless milk and eating tasteless eggs and tasteless beef. I noticed that Lucas would compliment every single meal his mother cooks - after he gobbled it in one blink, he would wash everything down with a glass of red wine and accompany it all with a loud burp. I would stare at him through the corner of my eye, wondering whether he meant what he had said, but the evidence that he did was written all over the empty plate in front of him. I'm a savvy woman, and I decided that complimenting was a habit I needed to acquire.

'This tastes really yummy, Mum,' I would say while learning how to use a knife and fork.

'Thank you, I'm glad you're enjoying it,' my kind-hearted mother-in-law would respond. My heart flips in guilt, knowing that – unlike my husband – I never meant it. I wonder whether my face is going to betray me.

'You want some more?' she enquires.

I excuse myself to the bathroom. I didn't want some more. As a matter of fact, I wanted to spit it all out — all of it. The bits that made it down to my stomach and the ones that were still fighting their way in, I want to spit them all in the bin. I rinse remnants out of my mouth with water. This would go on and on, and then there would be more and more. Food — the one thing that all human beings look forward to, something that gives us energy so that we can look forward to other things — this same food became something to dread.

In all these nightmares, I wonder where my people are – the African people who look like me. Do they exist here, or am I alone in this place? Where are they? Now, because I am married into a White family, and living in a White suburb, I have hardly seen any Black Africans. My sourness in this beautiful-looking city grows and swells. Soon it will become so large that I am unable to contain it, and then it will explode where the whole world would see it and know that I am truly not happy in this place.

Christmas has become no different to an ordinary day for me. The first Christmas I spend in Australia, I am looking at everybody and wondering when we were going to start, because apart from the kids opening presents and turkey roasting in the oven, nothing else is happening. Then evening comes and I hear my mother-in-law say, 'Oh, that was a great Christmas.'

I wonder if it is a time difference thing, which I still haven't fully gotten hold of. Surely we hadn't had Christmas. I want her to tell me that Christmas isn't finished. All I did was sit next to a tree called *the Christmas tree* in a living room called *the Christmas room* with my hands nicely tucked between my thighs. I had Christmas hats on and Christmas pyjamas, but that was about it. Surely it can't be the end of this Christmas.

I wonder when I had signed away my day of joy, the one big thing that every Nigerian cherishes. The event that shakes the nation and put smiles on the faces of both old and young. Christmas unites families and friends and neighbours. Where I come from, Christmas fells the biggest cows and rattles the fattest bank account until it is empty. Christmas comes with a certain energy in Nigeria, one that is unique and memorable and only accessed once in an entire year. All of that, I have now traded for life in Australia.

'I'm dead, Mummy,' I cry over the phone. I walk her through the horrible situation I have found myself in. I want her to get it, but she doesn't understand.

I have sacrificed so much; how much more? Love gifted me the privilege of being here. None of my family members have even left the country where I come from. I am aware of this, yet I whinge. Does it make me ungrateful if I am whinging about an opportunity that many would die for? But what use is this opportunity if it does not permit me to pursue my passion? I can trade many things but certainly not that. My hunger has blinded me. Even in the broad daylight it speaks to me, and I can't pretend that I don't hear it.

In time, I start to notice my people. They are here. But they are in the healthcare field, a total opposite of where I want to be. Some are carers, some are nurses or other service professionals. None of these jobs attract me. Which is ironic, because when I was little, when I was asked what I wanted to do when I grew up, my answer was always nursing. But my answer had nothing to do with the profession. I was drawn to the uniforms. They were breathtaking, especially those of the UBTH nursing students: well-ironed gowns that finished just above the knees, fitted black belt, flat black shoes and a pristine white hat, just like an Emirates air hostess. I didn't want to know what the work really entailed, I just knew the uniform would look perfect on me. The scrubs I see nurses wear in Australia only confirms that it had been the uniform that I was interested in all along, not the profession.

Many of the Africans I saw in those jobs didn't appear happy. Maybe it's just me, but I thought they all looked sad, even when the sky was blue. Some were pushing wheelchairs and I wondered if that was hard work. Surely there must be Black Africans in the other fields, healthcare isn't the only industry in Australia. They can't all be nurses and carers. I continue to look for at least one person in a different field: someone with long, fitted sleeves and nice pants; someone in news presenting or journalism or accounting; even law. Anything with fashion and style. A Black African wearing high-waisted pants that looked like they could kick ass.

There was nothing. Absolutely nothing.

Although I can't quite place my hands on what it is yet, I know something isn't right. My heart starts to race, and not in a positive way. I have met danger and I know what I'm going to do. I'm about to run. But going back to Africa is not an option – that would be the dumbest thing, even though the little sense in me knows that I cannot stay. Here I am, a 22-year-old woman with a permanent visa to live in one of the most beautiful countries in the world, yet I can't settle. I can't suck it up and face life like others are doing.

My worry increases even more after I am introduced to an African by my mother-in-law as her way of linking me with my community. This African woman advised me that nursing is my best option.

I am not a nurse. I am many things, but they are all to do with TV. Telling stories is the only thing I have ever wanted, and I can't sit and call it quits without even trying. What faces me in Australia is a challenge. But I have decided that it is now or never - this is my time; my moment! While my legs are still long and my body is still straight.

If it cannot be this, then it will be nothing and I will run.

Chapter 3: Hollywood

LA is perfect: the street is bustling and the air smells like an Oscar award. It is exciting to be here.

This place feels like a place for me, no doubt about it. Walking on the Hollywood Walk of Fame and seeing all the incredible names of people that I have only watched on my TV back home, it all makes it feel like I am getting close to finally achieving that dream of mine. I have come across countless film sets since I arrived. I have money, a great apartment right next to Griffith Observatory and a husband that is rooting for me.

Lucas offered me the gift of exploring my passion in the Unites States. I wouldn't say it's how I imagined it – as a person from a poor background, imagining Hollywood is like a person born male trying to get pregnant. My mind only stretched to the four corners of our cracked walls. But I have imagined talking like the White people, and now I am here, waiting to see my dream come true. I'm in a good place and I can't fuck it up. My family back home is depending on me for survival. Lucas is filling that responsibility for me at the moment, but I'm aware that he won't be doing it forever. I had better hurry up and get my shit together.

Hollywood feels like a place I can call home. It's got more Black people, and they walk freely on the street. Nobody turns to stare at them. In Australia, White people would turn and look at every single Black person that walks past as if they're an alien – like they've never seen a Black person before, even though they live on Black land. Plus, here, Black people do exist in the media. Lupita Nyong'o has just won an Academy Award for *12 Years A Slave*, so I think it's really promising here.

And oh, the food. The food here is great. They've got the best Carl's Jr. burgers and California cheesecake and Thai cuisine. Their restaurants have pictures so that when you order food, you know exactly what it is going to look like, which is great for a person like me who's new to Western foods. Australia doesn't have this and I hate it. I would order food like a blind person, constantly getting tripped up by guessing at what I'm ordering.

Every day, my confidence swells in this place, and I am very certain that it won't be long before my family starts seeing me on TV. I want to make my mum proud, and Lucas too, for sponsoring this dream. I'm going to make that happen.

I have signed up for Actors Access, a platform where audition calls are put out. I am impressed at the number of roles that seek Black actors — in Australia, no one seeks Black actors because it's a White media industry. Since I discovered Actors Access, I am swimming through it every day and applying for as many auditions as possible.

At these auditions, I realise that I need to have headshots. I am very new to the world of acting, so most of these words are new to me. I book to have my headshot done with a highly recommended photographer at $750 per hour – expensive, but I am after something that will get my foot in the door. If a headshot is what it takes, then this photographer can have my money.

'It's going to be worth it, I promise you,' the photographer brags as he turns and spins my head around for a shot. He sure looks like he knows what his doing, positioning me and provoking facial expressions that I didn't know I had.

'Casting directors wanna see that you're more than just a pretty face. They wanna see a range of emotions; that you can be angry, that you can be fierce, that you can be all of it and your headshot is where you've got that chance to show it,' he continued in his American accent. I would come to respect his professional skills more as the years pass and those headshots stay relevant.

Now that I have my headshots – and not just any headshot but stunning headshots that every person pauses to look at – I am back to audition applications, and I am certain that I am going to win a role soon. I attend the first, the second, the third… I am not getting any callbacks. But I'm not giving up, it's too early to do that. Then boom, I land a callback – in fact I had just finished auditioning with dozens of people, and they asked me and only a few others to wait. It's a good sign, right?

Soon, a White lady who looks like a model walks in and ushers me into an office. There's a guy in there. 'Congratulations,' he cheers, 'you are one of the few people that made it!' The butterfly inside my stomach startles. I knew this dream was going to come but oh boy, this quick? 'Fill in this form and sign it, and then we can proceed to the next stage.' Without knowing what the form said, I filled it in and signed.

I had just signed myself in as student at Barbizon Modeling and Acting School. Through their fishing hook, they reeled me in until I could not escape. I was in their net, handing in my dollars along with their other victims. It was easy to fall into their trap – Beyoncé and Lady Gaga attend the studio next to theirs, and they've got photos of incredible actors whom they claimed to be their students on display, so it was easy to be caught. And I thought people claiming to be Nigerian Princes were the biggest scam artists.

The Barbizon cage cost me six months of my time in America. By the time I was released, I had forgotten why I came to Hollywood in the first place. My best friend Iram, whom I met through Barbizon, has a degree and a job. So do other people that I am meeting in the world of acting. Acting is just a side thing for them, so their lives don't entirely depend on it. Mine does, and so does that of my family. I have to make a decision and I have to do it fast.

I have learned that behind all those famous people we saw on TV back home, there are many whose dreams ended up in the mud. I learned that not all that glitters is gold, and that people like Lupita Nyong'o didn't just get there overnight – she worked and she was put up against millions of other hungry actors. Taking a chance at Hollywood is like betting your life on lottery; the chances are slim.

I have a new plane ticket for Australia, but I don't know where I am going. I weep as I fasten my seatbelt because I'm leaving a land that holds my dreams, and yet my dreams did not recognise that I had come for them. I weep knowing that it would take just one of those auditions that I had attended to call me and say that they would sponsor my visa. I weep for my poor widowed mother who has been waiting for the day her daughter would make it and return home. I weep because I am getting older and I am unable to define my direction in life. I weep for every person who's ever had a dream which circumstances won't allow them to achieve.

My return to Australia is the right thing to do. I will go back to suffer its cold hands and endure its sharp teeth. I'll get my life together and get serious for once. I assure myself that I will accept what is, and let go of what isn't. What will be is whatever Australia hands me, and what isn't is only my dreams. I told myself this and although it sounded easy in my head, carrying it out becomes a problem.

Chapter 4: Now What?

I am back to do what is needed: acquire an education, like every other person in the Ottah family. My father taught me that education is the key, and even as he lays nine feet underground, he hasn't been proven wrong. He did it, his siblings did it, my siblings are doing it – it is only right that I do it.

It's been weeks since I returned and I'm yet to set my eyes on a camera, let alone film set. I get irritated at everything around me, and I wish it was different.

'Mum says you don't smile,' Lucas would say.

I'm afraid that I am tasting my first share of depression. Australia feels lonelier than I used to know it. As I roam around the streets, the people smile as they pass, but in their eyes is loneliness. I see lots of buried dreams – dreams that never got to see the beautiful sunlight of Australia because they've been traded for what is 'necessary', like families and children and responsibilities. Like mine. People are just surviving here, they are not living. They walk sluggishly, unfulfilled. I fear that this will become my fate, and as much as I don't want that, it seems to be the reality. The entire world appears dark, even in the brightest part of the day. I feel strange. As if my heart is sinking. As if I am waiting for permission to be happy without my dreams.

'Visit Nature,' Lucas urges. He has been trying everything he can to make me see that it isn't the end for this dream of mine. 'Just relax. It'll come.'

I wish I had that kind of faith. It is my dream, yet his faith seems to be larger than mine. There was never a day when he believed that it was over, even in the worst moments.

'Nature would do you a lot of good,' he soothes. Lucas cares, but I fail to see it. I chuckle and wonder what the fuck nature has to do with any of this.

'Nature will help you gain clarity.' Apparently Lucas is a nature freak. He believes that the god we pray to is Nature. He believes that healing and fulfillment come from Nature. He believes that Nature is pure in heart and in spirit, and is merciful and kind and compassionate. He believes that Nature cleanses. Lucas inhales Nature and exhales Nature. Nothing is as healing for him as taking a barefoot walk on cold, quiet beach sand. He cuddles seashells and pats the rocks. Lucas believes they are pure. Even in the coldest winter, he would beat the sunrise to the beach with his surfboard and breathe Nature.

Lucas says that Nature speaks quietly, and you can only hear it when your heart is quiet too. I'm a Nigerian woman, brought up in a country where more than 200 million people roam the streets. We don't know Nature. Our bushes are burned every year. From where I lived, going to the ocean was like taking a flight to Australia – and with so much litter around, it was as dirty as a public toilet. I had only visited the beach twice at the most in more than twenty years of African life.

Lucas's talks about Nature sound like gibberish to me. He and I have a lot of differences, but even the difference in our skin colour does not come close to the differences in our belief systems. I'm beginning to feel like Lucas is the cause of all the bad things. He is trying to help but overdoing it and I feel like I should strangle him. Seeing him every day makes me want to throw up. He hasn't done anything wrong, yet I am mad and upset, as if this was all his fault.

Months pass and I still don't know where I belong. Since I bundled my red carpet dresses and runway heels into a suitcase, I've become desperate. I applied for a cleaning service role which I got, and I am now sitting in an agency room for induction training, along with all the others who look like me and who are here for the same reason.

A White Australian woman joins us and preaches about how to become a professional cleaner. I listen as she rambles on and on.

Nothing is sinking in. I can see her lips moving and hear the sounds, but I can't make sense of what she's saying.

I smile as I hear her say the word 'bucket' as *backet*. She pronounces 'home' with her nose, to make it sound like *hoim*. Perhaps this hasn't been a complete waste of time. She makes it easy to catch onto the accent, unlike my husband and in-laws. Even after two years with them, I can say the word 'butter' ten times in my thick Nigerian accent, but my English mother-in-law still struggles to understand me. I haven't been able to catch the trick of how they say their words.

My charcoal-coloured skin is already enough of a barrier to belonging in this place. I need to acquire the acquirable.

The rest goes in one ear and filters through the other then settles in the bin. When the lecture about how to become an award-winning cleaner from a woman who's never done cleaning is finished, she asks if anyone has a question. I see hands being put up in the air. The class is filled with questions. I wonder what it is about cleaning that anyone would want to get further clarification on. Flush the toilets and clean the poos and wear gloves so you don't end up with poo in your mouth, how is there anything else?

We've been listening to this woman for hours, yet these people feel that isn't enough. They have been taking notes with exercise books and pens since the class began. I didn't even bring paper. I couldn't care less, which makes me start to wonder why I came in the first place.

I've been sitting at the very back, rolling my eyes and hissing the whole time. This is why they see Black Africans as dumb: others who look like me punch the woman with their numerous questions and in their eyes, I can see how much they need this. I can see that they haven't come here to waste two hours of their time on listening to an accent. They are focused and know exactly why they're here. I don't, and I don't think I care.

A couple of days after the cleaning job induction, a letter shows up in our mailbox. It is my new photo ID. I am to have an ID tag with me whilst flushing White people's toilets and wiping their basins and sinks. I hold it close to my face and stare at the person in this photo for a few minutes. The only thing that screams out to me is that the person in this photo isn't a cleaner. I share the news with Lucas, who thinks I'm ridiculous for applying in the first place.

'This is not who you are,' he states confidently.

'Well, this is what every African does here.'

'You're not every African.'

He says this continuously and I start to wonder whether I needed glasses to see what sets me apart from the rest of the Africans whose survival relies on scrubs and mops.

Every night, while the whole house snores, I am wide awake, thinking of things I have no control over. Thinking of the stakes and the man I'm committed to, who flew me all the way from Africa to this place. His family, who wholeheartedly welcomed me without question. My one year old son, whom I do not feel like a mother to.

I am a 24-year-old woman with no direction, thinking of my own poor, widowed mum and the siblings I've left behind, all relying on me for survival. The stakes are high. I may be young, but I am not too young to know that Lucas will not be helping my family forever. It is only wise that I prepare for when he changes his mind.

I visit a career adviser so that I can hear what the system thinks of me. I am sitting on the other side of the table, but the adviser positions the laptop well enough so that I see what he is talking about. Even when I am trying to change the topic or switch to other courses, testing what has been said, he is constantly trying to bring me back to where he thinks I belong based on the colour that sits in my skin. All of the available jobs in healthcare spit at me from his laptop.

He is right. I am a Black African, and nursing is where I belong. The evidence is written all over the job chart on the laptop. I sigh and take my leave.

I feel at peace, as though all the fighting is over – and it is. I am ready to surrender, and as much as this makes me feel sad, it is the only choice. If it guarantees my family's survival, I'm all in. My mother has medical conditions that constantly call for emergency assistance. My brother is in university, and he cannot complete it without my support. Other family members are still in school.

Studying nursing promises to do more good than harm. I would be financially independent, which means I can finally take charge of providing for my family. This also means that I can stay here and be a mother to my son and my two step-children, who are also calling me 'Mum'. And I get to enjoy my wonderful mother-in-law's food. The meals I used to hate are now my favorites. In fact, there is nothing I look forward to more than her delicious Sunday Roast chicken, her cauliflower cheese, and creamy mashed potato with gravy. Red wine has become our water. Every evening, we chill in our backyard, sipping on wine with nibbles while we wait for the barbecue to be ready.

We are the Baileys. If burying my passion is the only sacrifice to make here, then so be it.

Chapter 5: Join Them

Every day here is a nightmare. Time doesn't move when you're doing something that you don't love. I am working on a Cert IV in Health Service Assistance, which is said to lead me directly into nursing if I pass my exams - a path that I'm clearly not going to use. Something inside me tells me that this isn't the way, yet I choose to play deaf. Instead of listening to myself, I'm filling my ears with medical gibberish like 'syringe this' and 'syringe that' and 'anti-this' and 'anti-that' with my eyes glued to a wall clock. It's sickening, and there is not a day that goes by that I don't wonder what I am doing here – but each time I question myself, the answer remains the same. *You don't take medicine because you like to, you take it because you are unwell.*

I close my eyes and chew that medicine like a sick person would. I get it. I'm taking it, Australia.

I have made a few friends, and I'm beginning to take note of the different racial groups; we have lots of Asians, lots of Africans and few Caucasians. The Caucasians are here because they want to be here. Some of the Africans are here because they feel they have to be here. Many of the Asians are here because they already worked in the field before they moved to Australia, and they're only here to strengthen their accreditation. I'm a lost sheep, waiting to be navigated. I doubt I even know myself at this point.

Doing something that you're not passionate about is as good as being in prison – in fact, I don't see any difference between myself and a prisoner. At least they've got some air; I am practically suffocating. I always look forward to lunchtime because then I can escape. I get to chat like the parrot that I am, telling stories and making my companions feel something. Lunchtime is where I get to reconnect with myself and re-evaluate my passion for storytelling, making sure that I've still got what I used to have. Every single time, I am reassured of who I am and yet every single time, I choose to live in denial.

'You are very good at storytelling, Jess,' my classmates compliment.

'You should seriously consider art,' another suggests. I chuckle and sigh. I have heard this before. The same words whisper in my ears when I zone out, recalling similar moments with my secondary school friends.

We receive our nursing scrubs. I am starting to wonder how I'm going to continue with this path in baggy pants and oversized shoes. I no longer wear makeup, which is certainly not me. I'm getting deeper into this than I expected and wondering how I am going to swim. I'm baffled by the fact that everyone else seems to be happy about this. Surely they're not faking it – but if they are, I need their trainer because they're doing a pretty good job.

One minute, I have convinced myself to move on; the next, I am on StarNow, an online platform for media talent. I'm creating a profile and chasing after auditions that do not call for Black people, looking like a fool each time I attend. I'm really confused. I'll check that website over months and years, hoping that someone would create a story that demands Black people. I am constantly taking pictures and videos of myself and everything I do.

Lucas has bought a new camera, and whenever we're out at the beach I am busy filming and creating stories. I wake Lucas in the middle of the night, asking him to please take my picture because I have a story idea that would suit the light in our room. 'Make sure you don't put the rest of the family online,' Lucas would warn, and I agree. He takes my pictures, but I always repay his favours.

I am myself in these moments. This is the place where I shine.

I juggle myself between two worlds. Months pass while doing my course: I go to class every day, I listen to lectures and attend tutorials, yet I couldn't tell you if I learned anything. I remember needles, I remember dosage and drugs, but that's pretty much it.

I am not worried about succeeding at my nursing entrance exams, even though they keep going on about how competitive it is. I figured out how to cram for papers in secondary school. If I can pass my exams it means I can graduate, and if I'm able to graduate it means I can get a job and earn money. What am I complaining about? I have to suck it up. My younger brother has two years to go before graduating and my mum and siblings are already counting down to when I'm going to get a job.

I thought my passion was all that needed to be sacrificed for this path. I thought wearing big shoes and oversized scrubs that I never liked was the end of it. But no. I surrendered to the nursing path so that my family can live. Now it seems that this path wants more and this time, the motherfucker wants my life.

I am doing my prac at St John of God Hospital as part of the requirements for my course. I am in the hallway with my eyes glued solidly to a different wall clock, sitting opposite the reception desk. I wait for time to move so that I can go for my lunch escape.

A group of my fellow students are marching forward, all wearing smiles on their faces. I wonder what their excitement is about.

I pull one of them aside. "Where are you guys headed?"

'To the morgue,' she smiles.

I don't think I heard that right. 'The what?'

'The morgue,' she smiles again.

'To see dead people?'

I let go of her hand, chuckling to offset my discomfort.

One of the things I love about Australia is that it hides the existence of deaths from its citizens. I know that deaths are happening, but they are not in my face. Here, the images of dotted blue and white coffins from my home village of Isumpe are starting to fade. But today I am being told that if I must stay on this path – the same path I have sacrificed my passion for – that I must come face to face with dead bodies.

Death and bodies and coffins were my biggest fear when I was growing up. I know death happens everywhere, but in Nigeria, death pours down like rain. The local cemetery was located next to our house, meaning that I would know the exact number of deaths that occurred each week. Local families who didn't have money would bring their deceased loved ones with a bicycle. The ones who were well-off would use a car. Every day, if it's not bicycles and screaming family members bringing dotted blue-and-white coffins, then it is a car siren screaming. Each time I could see or hear them coming, I would run straight to my house and jam the door shut, panting in fear. And as if that is not enough, these sounds and images would follow me into my dreams.

When I was young, I asked my mother if we could relocate to a place where people don't die, because I didn't want to die and I didn't want her to die either.

My mother looked at me. 'Ifelunwa, there is no place where people don't die.' I looked into her eyes, wondering if she was joking. She was not.

The fact that no one I knew could provide an answer to my questions about death made me fear it all the more.

It is now my life which is at stake. Yvonne, my supervisor, has warned that I have gotten away with not attending the current mortuary visits, but I would not get away with it in a job.

If I am to see a dead body, they'll need to bury me first.

Chapter 6: No Shortcut

At the age of 11, I wrote my first story. It was about a teenage girl who got caught up with bad friends and ended up pregnant. She kept her parents in the dark until her condition became an emergency which ended her life.

I did not leave Nigeria without it.

When I moved to Australia in 2012, I was so excited to work with my passion for storytelling. Each time I looked through the window, all I could see were things that whispered stories into my ears; the trees, the ocean, even the birds, all yearning for their stories to be told. But when I turned on the television and did not find a single person who look like me in there, I weakened. I understood that there was an unwritten code, and it was bold. I realized that under this bright blue sky was a devourer, one that is not merciful to a skin colour like mine.

I created a story about a young African woman called Olivia who has been diagnosed with a brain tumor while she is fulfilling her long-term dream of receiving an Australian visa for her family. Olivia becomes caught between continuing that goal or quitting for death. The feature-length script was done as a Microsoft Word document - anyone who writes scripts would know how time consuming this is, yet it took me less than a month. A passion is the only thing you do with ease, even when you're not getting paid.

Lucas was part of the process. Whenever I'd get stuck, I would use him as my sounding board. 'What if Olivia's mum visits and Olivia sees her before she closes her eyes?'

'Good' he would say. 'Maybe make the siblings come as well and have Jake get them a permanent visa.'

'Great idea, I never thought of it that way!'

Later on, Lucas told me he didn't like the script. He was skeptical about the fact that Olivia's story is dark. He noticed that I'm very fond of dark stories and didn't like that side of me. He wanted me to write things that make people laugh, or uplifting stories with hope. He didn't know that the stories I tell are stories that have been lived around me. But I know what he is saying, so I get him to cool down while I figure out how to get him to buy into what I am doing.

Bringing *Olivia* to life is the next natural thing to do. I've never met anyone in the film industry here in Australia, but I do have contacts in Nigeria. I decide to reach out to the directors who have made my favourite movies. I am desperate at this point. I really want to get on TV and this story is my ticket, because I wrote it for me to be the lead actress. Once I make this movie, people are going to be watching me. Then I'll write another and another and continue to star in them, then maybe travel to Nigeria and start featuring in other people's movies. Africans in Africa respect people from abroad, especially after they've acquired foreign accents. In a few years, this will be me and the struggle would be over. I would kiss Australia goodbye forever and I won't need any more education because I will be too famous to care.

I really like one of the directors that I have made contact with. Emmanuel is humble, but he is also a Gemini like me and very creative – I have watched his movies and they are good. He's thrilled with the idea of coming to Australia. He had been praying and fasting for his work to take him places right before I made contact with him. To him, it seems like it is a prayer answered.

Emmanuel wonders why I would live in such a privileged space and I have not yet made anything. This is very un-Nigerian to him. Nigerians are so ingenious that if life gives them lemon, they can make lemonade.

'It is not that simple,' I cry to him. He wants more explanations but I stumble. I can't find the words to articulate the fact that Black people like myself don't have a space in Australian media; we exist, but can't be part of it like other Australians. 'You would have to be here to see it, so you can understand for yourself.'

In response, Emmanuel ties it to laziness and lack of ambition. Very un-Nigerian indeed.

Emmanuel's visa is processing, and every day I imagine my name at the end of film credits. Mama would be proud.

Staring Jessica Bailey and Written by Jessica Bailey.

The excitement of fulfilling my dream turns me into a salesperson. I start to pitch Olivia's story to every stranger I meet. I tell them how the story is about to come to fruition and how it has been my dream to tell stories and be featured on the screen. I tell them my experience with Australia and how I hadn't set my eyes on a camera since I arrived, and how that weighed on me. But not anymore, because I am about to ship a camera all the way from Nigeria. Everyone I talk to admires my courage and commitment. However, of all those people I have pitched the story to, only one of them came back: Simon.

I share more while having a coffee with him: how I want to return to Nigeria so that I can pursue my passion, and how I have planned for a Nigerian filmmaker to come here to Australia to bring my story to fruition.

'I like your story, and the way you tell it,' Simon says. 'You're a very intelligent young woman. Australia has a lot for you. Why don't you study your craft at university here, where you can polish that skill and also gain a network of people from your class who could potentially support you in making your film?' Simon pushes at me with these facts and suddenly I go blank. I thought I had it all together, but suddenly it feels like I don't know what I was doing. This is sounding like it's sending me back to square one, where I don't want to be because I am already progressing with a plan. I don't need this lecturing from a man I don't even know, but by the time Simon finishes his words, I am paralysed.

Chapter 7: Dilemma

During my secondary school years, my uncle made me pick a science course. My peers and I were taught to believe that art class is for the unintelligent, and this was the philosophy we lived by. Even mingling with the art students was classified as *living backwards*. My uncle could have disowned me for that, he was that strict.

African parents think they own the keys to the ground you walk on, simply by being your parents. My late uncle played the father figure to my brother and I after my dad passed, and he decided it was either nursing or nothing for me; my passion could not hold water.

The decision to stay in science class suffocated the living daylights out of me. English and Literature were my favorite subjects at school, and that made Mrs Agamu, my English and Literature teacher, my favorite. Mrs Agamu was a charmer. Men admired her well-round backside and students like me worshipped her proficiency with the English language. Mrs Agamu would read with passion and confidence. Each time I heard her eloquent voice drift from the classroom next door and through the open roof of my science class as she read *The Gods Are Not to Blame*, my heart would flip, reminding me that I made the wrong decision.

In the nursing entrance exam, I sit with my pen running down the paper, filling the blank pages by vomiting lies about my passion for nursing, where it comes from and how well I looked after my paternal grandmother (who died long before I was born).

Thinking about this, I can finally see that I have not been the one in control of my life. I decide that, once and for all, I must learn to distance myself from the people who once stood in the way of my stories.

I consider starting filmmaking studies at UWA, as Simon suggested. It's looking good, but I am a bit scared of university in Australia. I could not even make it into university in Nigeria. I was living away from my mother by the time I finished secondary school, making very little money. I still paid and sat for many entrance exams, but I never made it through, even by the time my peers were in their final years.

I submit my application to UWA anyway.

I receive an offer for filmmaking and an offer for nursing, and suddenly I become more conflicted than I ever was. I go for a walk every day, reviewing both offers and doing more research. Google has told me many times that there's no African-Australians in filmmaking. I know that there are no filmmaking jobs in Australia for me, yet I'm still searching.

It's as if I don't know what to choose, or maybe I do but my fear for financial security won't let me admit it. I worry that my family in Nigeria are still heavily depending on me. Nursing promises a better life for them; filmmaking promises nothing. Three years is a lot of time, and the money for such expensive fees won't be offered twice. It is a big risk to dedicate myself to a degree where the certificate might only be as good as toilet paper. If I blow this up, that's it.

At the same time, my home is no longer what it used to be. Lucas is no longer working; money is starting to run out. He blames everybody for everything that goes wrong in his life: his parents, and me and the children. We can never be too careful. No matter how hard we try, something must go wrong, and he'll start yelling and swearing. It swells the whole house with noise. He is starting to meet with his demons, and they're not backing down. Money running low seems to trigger them even more.

If it all sinks and Lucas and I separate, I have nowhere to go to. I have no one here. No family, nothing. Not even friends, really. I am as alone as I have ever been. Not having financial independence leaves me a slave to the abuse that has crept into my home.

I really need to buckle my shit up very quickly. Most importantly, I need to make a good decision. We all know what the good one is at this point. I must pick nursing, unless I want to be selfish and leave my family to die of hunger. I need something that will also allow me to survive.

My mind is made up to hit the *enter* key on the nursing offer. But then Lucas looks me in the eyes and says, 'Whatever decision you make, I'll support you.' All of my thoughts about financial independence vanish. I suddenly feel that sense of security and protection again, the same one a child gets from their parents. I felt it when we first met.

That day in Ghana, I told him my story about being kicked out of my uncle's home in Nigeria, and how my mother became ill soon after I left. He gave me his credit card to withdraw money that I could send to her, and he did not put a limit on how much.

Lucas promised to get help so that we no longer fight. He looks like he means it.

Although things start to balance out when I begin studying, I still don't feel like university has a place for me. I am tempted to quit and return to my home country, especially with the constant fighting around the house. Lucas's demons have returned, and they have grown in size and in number.

Every day, I am spilling all my problems into Simon's ears, but I feel like he's not getting it, and I want him to. I am afraid, and this time it's not just the normal fear of navigating through life. My biggest fear is wasting three years on a degree that will get me nowhere in Australia.

I come from a country that has a booming film industry, and I don't need a degree to break in. I have read so many stories of Nigerian expats like me who returned and never looked back. These people break into the industry straightaway and feature in at least ten movies a year. I've lived in Australia for couple of years now. I have a little Western accent coming through, and my skin has been brightened by the Australian sunlight. I am the package they want back in my country.

Simon is so articulate—he puts his words together so well that they are hard to fight. Simon reveals all of Nigeria's wounds and I'm left wondering whether I can even call it home. He tells me about the non-stop crime wave that swarms Nigeria. He tells me about its broken government. He tells me about the poverty and hunger that roams the streets.

Simon even goes as far as digging into Nollywood, which I speak so highly about. He tells me how poor the industry is, with payments so low they don't sustain the workers. I am shocked and stuck to my spot. Is this the same Nollywood that I see? The Nigerian celebrities that I follow on social media are rich, they are a big deal! The men drive flashy cars while the women rock handbags by Louis Vuitton – surely they're not faking. I try to counter his points but Simon no longer patronises me; he is here to give me sound words of advice, like a father would. He says it is up to me to whether to take it or not.

I am embarrassed and disappointed. I want him to stop. I feel like I have nowhere to go to, like an orphan. I feel like this man hates me, like he deliberately came to ruin my life… but a part of me still wants his approval, like a child waiting to hear kind words from their mother.

'You are making the wrong decision,' he says. 'My advice is: get that film degree, and then travel if you want. That way, you've got background knowledge from a recognized institution. If you leave, you might lose this opportunity. If you stay, it's only three years and before you know it, you're there.' He suddenly asks me, 'What are you afraid of?'

I'm muted. He has this effect on me, every time.

Chapter 8: White Faces

Children growing up in Nigeria are made to see White people as extraordinary. Before I left home, I had never seen a White person - although I had heard many stories about them. I think most of those must have been cooked up, because the people who fed us those stories had never seen a White person themselves. The story is always that they have a friend who knows a friend that knows a friend that knows White people... Even though we knew these stories weren't entirely true, we believed them because we were fascinated. They always painted the reputations of White people so high that they make you think that White people are second to Jesus, and that the rest of us are not worthy of even the shoes that they walk in.

We were also taught that the thing which looks to be the size of a toy that flies loudly in the air is called *airplane*, and it belongs to the White people. You should have seen the shock in our eyes when they told us that it carries White people every time it passes. I didn't believe it. I would try to imagine it but seemed impossible to me. For all I knew, White people might not even be real. The tiny little thing that looked like an ant in the air, how could it accommodate even one person? If it went on the clouds, did that mean the White people inside have seen God? I didn't want to believe it but I couldn't let the ideas go.

A plane whizzed past our yard once a month, so my cousins and I would run, calling after it with bare feet and ripped underpants.

Aeroplan go se numu buread o!
Aeroplan go se numu buread o!

'Airplane, buy me bread.' We would sing with all of our muscles and passion, voices raised to the maximum and desperately wishing they would hear us. We would run and run, singing in chorus until we ran out of breath and strength, but we still wouldn't stop until the plane became completely buried in the sky and we lost sight of it.

As I grew, my curiosity about White people never left me, and the more I dug, the more confirmation I got that White people are truly second to Jesus. Yet, here I am in a lecture class, receiving the same lecture as the White people and I am to apply this same knowledge in the same way within real life. It feels like some kind of joke. I'm sure I don't belong here.

My loneliness builds. There's no one to talk to in class because I haven't got the same skin colour or the same accent as anyone else. I haven't got long hair either. A lot seems to be working against me. It gets worse when I realise that everything except for lectures and tutorials are all online, via *LMS*. I don't know what LMS is – in fact, I don't know much at all about computers. Nigerian parents usually enroll their children for computer training after they've completed secondary school, but my uncle overlooked that because of the cost and I can't blame him. He had done enough for my brother and I.

The talk of LMS language is increasing in my classes. Somebody coughs, they say 'LMS'. A person sneezes, I hear 'LMS'. It sounds complicated to me and the more I hear it, the more I panic. It seems like it is going to be the make-or-break factor. We're in Week Three and people are already submitting their assignments using LMS and I haven't even started mine because I don't know how to access them. I am afraid to interact with other students to ask questions because I don't look like them. What was I thinking? It's time to quit. I'm a fucking goddamned Black woman and I can never belong in this place.

Eventually, I find LMS. My assignments score High Distinctions and best of all, the comments from my peers and lecturers about my presentation skills have been encouraging. Everyone says they love the way I present, just as my Nigerian classmates used to.

Hearing it from qualified university lecturers and other White faces makes a big difference. I start to hone in on this and see how I can continue using it to my advantage, such that my skills would mask the colour of my skin and possibly win White faces to my side.

Semester One finally ends, and I am still living with confusion, wondering why I can't make up my mind. It is killing me! I'm in my mid-20s but I can't get my act together. I'm a mother of one, yet my child seems more responsible than I am. I can't even get a simple driver's license – my mother must have offended someone! I am starting to wonder whether this is a test, or whether people in my village have something to do with it, because I don't understand.

With all that is going on, I am happy that I still have people backing me. Lucas strongly believes that I am greater than I think I am. Every time I feel low to the point of quitting, he says, 'You have no idea how powerful you are.' Simon has practically become a father – if I struggle for fees, Simon is ready to pay them. 'I've got your back,' is all he would say.

This is a rare privilege, and I won't take it for granted. I am committed to getting that degree. I have completed one semester, which means I'm six months down the track of the three-year journey. Simon was right, it goes fast. I want to ignore whatever distractions there are and smash this.

Chapter 9: Run!

"I'm not keeping him!" I cry out to Lucas when we sit down to discuss the situation. I am in my second year at uni and I'm pregnant. It wasn't planned. I am aware that after having one kid, the natural next step is to have a second – but not now! Not when I am starting to get a handle on my course. I can't take chances, uni is difficult enough for me. As a migrant from a very different culture, I put in triple the efforts compared to my peers. Adding pregnancy to this situation would surely crush this journey. I haven't got space for pregnancy.

Lucas is adamant that he wants me to keep the baby. 'You can continue with your studies, then after the delivery I'll look after him while you return to your classes," he urges.

Being a Black person in a White crowd bears a stigma and it causes stares, now being pregnant on top that will only increase my shame. I am not ready to face this.

Time is ticking. My cheeks are starting to swell and so are my boobs. The fact that I am three months gone means that I only have six months left to put up with this, should I decide to keep it. At the rate I'm going, I don't think there's ever going to be a good time to have another baby – this might be the only chance I have. All of these thoughts, coupled with Lucas's persistence, have me feeling like the best decision for me is to keep it.

With Lucas's support and encouragement, my fear suddenly disappears. I am rocking my pregnancy at uni confidently, doing fulltime with no apologies. By the end of my third semester, the baby is almost due. We schedule a C-section.

My second child has arrived and I did not feel a thing. I am not breastfeeding, just the same as with my first, so I bounced back to uni later that week like nothing ever happened. Lucas does as he said he would, looking after the baby. Everything is fine and I feel stronger by the day, but in a different kind of way. I start to feel more powerful, like those women who would have their jeans cut high and reverse the car without using the rearview mirror. I am a mother and expected to be soft, but I am quite the opposite. I have not one ounce of motherhood in me. The feeling is good.

The fighting and arguments at home grow into a war. Suddenly, I am feeling like a baby in this land, and I am in the middle of my studies, trying to find my feet and I need shoulders to lean on but home no longer feels like home and I no longer know what I am doing. My husband — the man whose words I've trusted from beginning, who took me on a journey to the other side of the ocean — lets go of my hands, and I wonder who will guide me. I weep and sob and wail and feel there is no one. We argue about everything: a day that didn't go well, food that got burnt by accident, the dishwasher that didn't wash properly, even the air-conditioner that fails to function as instructed; we argue about it all. If it were just the arguing I would stay, but there is more.

Lucas is starting to get physical, and I am terrified. This is no joke. One woman dies every week in Australia from domestic violence. This terrifies me the most. I could die and my family in Nigeria would not know. I am alone here.

The demons in us start to roar. All of the monsters inside both of us awaken and they are not backing down. They are hungry, waiting to see who would devour whom. There is physical rage in the house. It is no longer home. I knew we had reached the end when he starts picking objects at me while my children watched. I ran, and for the first time, this was a good kind of running. This was a run to save me, so that the family I have left behind on the other side of the world can see me again. This is a run to get that degree that I have worked hard for. I am not ready to die. This place is a No Man's Land. Things are not as rosy as they seem. Where I come from is far away and even if I screamed from that night until tomorrow, no one would hear me. It's a lonely place, I see that clearly now. I *run!*

I start looking for a place to stay nearby and manage to secure a room in a sharehouse. I am hardly there. It always feels like I'm a visitor. In the middle of the night, in my empty bedroom, I sob until there's nothing left in me. All I want to do is quit, but quitting seems as difficult as continuing. What if education isn't it? What if this path doesn't get me anywhere? I haven't got the luxury of getting it wrong. I don't know which path to follow. I wail until a voice inside me reminds me that I have been strong before. Then I remember: strong women do cry!

I moved without my children. Lucas has always been a good father to them. He is aggressive towards me, but he never tries it with the children, so I trust him to remain with them. Plus, I can only afford rent in a sharehouse and the kids cannot cope with that. I check on them two or three times a week and they look happy. They wonder what is going on. Sometimes we all eat dinner together.

Lucas can still be very caring towards me. In fact, sometimes he makes extra lunches and dinners for me to take away. But living away from my family does not stop the fights. Within those few hours that I visit, somehow Lucas always encounters a trigger. The moment he starts, I run to the car without saying goodbye to my children.

Simon assists me with rent. He is like a father to me; my only supporter in this lonely land. A Godsend. I wonder what and where I would be without him.

Simon is now in his sixties and has grey hair. He has proven that he is here to stay. He has seen something within me and he is here to help nurture it. I become a project for Simon, who works as a project manager. He seems so genuinely committed to watching me unleash the buried gifts that are inside me. At this moment, he is my one and only true friend. Rather than getting tired of hearing about all my troubles, Simon says, 'My life is really boring compared to yours. This is free entertainment for me.' Then he offers me advice.

I don't like Simon's advice. It is brutal. I'm the kind of person that wants what I want right now. Show me the shortest possible shortcut to get that dream, and there you'll find me. Simon is the opposite; he is all about process and strategy. I see why he came into my life, but I feel as if I haven't got time. I am getting old and I should be smashing my dreams by now, rather than strategising and planning. But as much as I hate Simon's advice and feel like letting him go, he helps me see bitter truths. Because of him, I can see that what I want to achieve requires strategy and plans. I see that it requires perseverance and commitment and hard work. I see that to become that incredible woman that I have always wanted to be, it comes down to how much I am willing to stick around.

Slowly but surely, something inside me wakes, and all of the energy I used for fighting, yelling, screaming and wailing at Lucas gets channelled into my studies. I study from morning to night. It becomes therapy. I also do it because it is all that I have now, and my marks could be the thing between me and my professional breakthough. I am getting High Distinctions, yet I am still bothered. If I graduate and don't get a job, then it will be time to return to my home country and accept my fate.

By the time I have one year left, quitting is not an option. I am no longer the only person involved in my decision, and I have decided that I'm not going to run any further because I have children in Australia. The only solution I have is to work hard, and I am prepared for that.

Strong women are not called *strong women* for nothing. Strong women go through fire, and it is through that process of burning that they become strong women. Strong women never ask for those fires, but they come. Challenges are always there, and they grow, but it is what you do with them. I could have quit, like I always do; I could have run like I did before. I didn't this time because maturity is coming to me. Life is getting more serious now, and I realise that one day there will be nowhere left to run to. If I'm able to tackle this obstacle, the next one will be easier – and there'll always be the next one.

Chapter 10: Not a Nurse

Getting a degree in a place like Australia is a dream for the people that I have left behind in my country. I should be happy, but I'm not.

Sitting and surrounded by a bunch of White faces, it is almost like being back at the first day of class. It feels good to be wearing the same gown as them with the hat seated on our heads. We'll all be receiving equal certificates. I am finally achieving the dream that my father and every member of my family wished for me.

Can someone put a bullet through my skull already?

'What did you study?' one of the guys seated beside me asks.

My heart flips. 'Uhh… film. Screen Production,' I stammer. I am a Black woman in Australia… I feel like I've wasted everything. What would a Black woman be doing with a degree in Screen Production in Australia? What was I thinking? The name of my course rings in my ears and makes me want to puke on myself. I feel chilled.

He says that he has studied photography. I wonder whether I could tap into one of his amazing plans. My tears build. I have wasted three years. Others can afford waste, but for a poor Black woman like me, it is stupidity.

The belief in my failure grows over time. I am constantly reminded of how useless my degree is. Every single day, I'm searching the internet for a job in my field with no good results. I have two children who are depending on me. I have more family back home who do not eat unless I send money. I have no real place to live here. I am in a strange country with a failed marriage.

My fear grows wild and wide. I wonder where to run to, whom to talk to. There is air, yet I struggle to breathe.

"Congratulations my darling", my mother-in-law cheers. My mother-in-law might be the nicest person I know, and she has supported me through my entire journey in Australia. Yet my heart struggles, because I know what will follow.

"So, what next?" There it is. There is the bullet I was expecting.

"Umm… get a job." I smile. "Start earning."

If I have failed, I am to be blamed. I was given an opportunity, yet I wasted it. I want them to crucify me. If they don't, I will do it myself.

I log onto Facebook, stalking my mates from nursing. Audrey and Harriet are doing well, paying mortgages and living responsibly with their families. Others are moving states and changing jobs as if it's nothing. I don't even have a job. I could have done nursing. I could have sucked it up like everyone else did. I feel completely useless. I am now taking the blame. I think it's no wonder that Lucas got fed up. At what was once my home, my children run up to me and call me Mum but I want to hide because I do not feel worthy of it.

Lucas and I fight, and he is no longer sending money to my family because he hasn't been working. A year ago, I started sharing my Student Allowance payments with them. Now that I am done studying, the payments will stop soon. I can't find a job. My mum is always sick but I can't afford to send her to a hospital. I stopped reaching out to them so that I don't hear their voices when they haven't eaten.

I start searching for health industry jobs again. Now I know why all the migrants I have come across are doing nursing. Now I see why we are not on TV. The reality of my situation is hitting me. I switch to searching for jobs in aged care. Boom, I get an interview.

'Tell us why you're suitable for this job.' This is the same as the questions I had in my nursing entrance examination. I remember that I'm a storyteller.

But this time it's for real, and if I get this job, I will be doing what they tell me. I look the interviewer in the eyes and go mute for a moment.

'I don't want this job. This job isn't me. I am not a carer. I am not a nurse.' I stand up and walk out the door.

'You are a lot of things, but you are definitely not a nurse,' Simon agrees. 'Think of where you were four years ago when I met you, and think of yourself now. You have grown, and you will continue to grow… You need to go to Nigeria.'

I am a broken woman, but suddenly I don't want to go to Nigeria. Simon pushes at me. 'You'll forever regret it if you don't. Especially if you think that you've missed out on things.' Simon talks like a psychic sometimes. I hate him for always being tough and strict and brutal yet he's the first person I run to when things go wrong. The one that hits me with truths so deep that they sound like déjà vu. 'I think your fear is playing with you again,' he says.

He's right. I have researched Nigeria since over the years, I know that it is not a good place to be. One hundred girls kidnapped in a day, two hundred people dead in a single crash. It is not a safe place, yet this man wants me to go. He says it's the only way I can see for myself what the industry really is.

What if I die? I have mixed feelings about that, if I'm telling the truth. My marriage with Lucas is still in the fire and I'm hardly spending any time with my children. It's as if my presence at the house is what starts the fire, and I am worried about my children witnessing fights between their parents every time they are together. I still don't have a job. I'm not even applying for jobs because there's none to apply for. The rent that I paid for six months will soon run out and I cannot guarantee that I am going to be able to pay more.

Bugger it, I am going to Nigeria.

My eye catches familiar green plantation trees when we descend into Lagos. Memories start to flash in my mind, and I feel that the teenager in me is staring at the person I am now, and my late uncle is there too — memories and stories all start to come back with emotions, swelling as large as the P-Square songs that pulse through my headphones. An uncontrollable tear rolls down my cheek and settles on my top. I want to return to the teenage girl and say that I am sorry - but I am not. I would not let her make me feel bad. I was young and innocent when I made the choices that led me away from here, and I will not be sorry for that. The clock never looks back.

I take a deep breath as I unbuckle my seatbelt. I look around and see Black faces, so I feel like I am home. I used to know these faces. It feels good but weird and confusing at the same time. As we make our way to terminal, a hot gust of air strikes my face. It is my first time experiencing this kind of air in a long time and I am gasping. I stand at the grungy airport carousel, waiting for my luggage to roll around. It is sweaty and sticky. I am already starting to regret my decision.

My luggage is not here. I panic because my laptop is in there, and I have researched enough about Nigeria to know that nothing is safe in this country, including myself. I could be snatched and nobody would care. My heart starts to beat faster. I am scared like never before and I am starting to wonder if I should stay. My mind is telling me to *bugger off* back to Australia because I clearly don't belong here anymore.

This is not how I imagined it from the other side of the ocean. It's been so long since I left. Everything seems strange, from the way the people stare to the way they laugh and the way they talk. I don't remember it this way. The loudness in their voices is difficult to process. I try to smile at people when my eyes meet with theirs, but they aren't responding. Smiling to say 'hi' is not part of the culture here, and I have lost knowledge of what is. I feel like a stranger in this place and for the first time, the meaning of the word *diaspora* becomes clear.

I'm lost and confused, the way I was on my first day in Australia. That day, my father-in-law came to pick us up from the airport with his green Mitsubishi. I remember staring at him from the back seat and wondering how best to greet him. It is that same feeling I'm having now, except I'm in my motherland.

I can't imagine how I would manage the disappointment of my godfather who is on his way right now to pick me up (if he's not already outside). My godfather lives in a different state, so he has travelled many kilometers to meet me. I can imagine how he would feel if I said that I am not staying even one night in this place.

Just as my panic becomes unbearable, there is my luggage. My phone rings, and it's my godfather outside. I rush to meet him at the exit. I am so sad, lost, and lonely. I am frustrated that I am staring at the man that knew me as a child, who hasn't seen me in twelve years, yet I want to leave him. I am sad because I am standing in the land that saw my birth and heard my first cry, watched me crawl and heard my first giggle, yet it pretends it does not know me. Tears drip from my cheeks, but they are only a few of the tears that are bubbling inside. I don't feel at home. I don't belong anywhere. I am lost.

A busted-up car drives toward us. Apparently it's a cab and we are meant to go in it. I look to my Godfather and chuckle. 'If you call this a cab, then I clearly don't belong here because what is before me shouldn't be travelling on the road, and if you and the country can't see that, and you approve of things like this, then the country and its citizens are sick.' I look to my right and my left, all the cabs that I see are the same as the one before us. The sun starts to go down, and it looks like it is going to rain. My Godfather is tired. I hop in.

I scan for a seatbelt and can't find one. I ask the cab driver where the seatbelt is and he says car isn't built with seatbelts at the back. I go bananas at him.

The car is singing mechanical songs as it moves, so I tell him to pull over and leave me because I need to go back to Australia. He directs my godfather to make me understand that this is Nigeria. Hearing that makes me feel even sicker. We keep driving away from the airport, my heart in my hands.

I am still expressing my frustration at the cab driver while he is receiving phone calls and driving on a highway with no speed limit. He speeds past a red light that might have turned black and then he turns into oncoming traffic and I wonder what is wrong with the people in Nigeria.

When we finally reach our stop, I take a shower in the AirBnB that my godfather rented for me which is clearly not what I ordered.

I am pissed at everything, too irritated to even share stories of the past twelve years with my godfather who is dying to hear them.

I have researched all the upcoming auditions in Lagos, and one of them is tomorrow at 10am. I ask my godfather how and when to leave the house to make it on time. He suggests leaving at 6am.

It's a journey that shouldn't have taken more than thirty minutes. But after three hours on the road, I am still not at my audition, cooking in an Uber that claims to have air conditioning. I eventually paid the driver and hopped out to meet a crowd of five hundred other candidates. I panic and pull one of them into a corner.

'Please, I'm here for an audition.'

'You're at the right place.'

'Who are all these people?'

'We're here for the same reason.'

I freak out, maybe I didn't hear her well. Did she just say five hundred actors are competing for this role?

Eight hours later, I am still here and it is not yet my turn. Only a few people have gone in, and I don't know what the problem is. We're all sweating with no food or water, getting distracted by some of the candidates fighting for one fan in a corner that is meant to service the entire hall. While everyone else seems to be used to the situation, I am starting to get concerned. I ask someone, 'What is really going on? Why haven't we auditioned?' People laugh at the worry on my face before they walk me through how it works here. They wonder what part of Africa I am from. Some guess Ghana, others say Kenya, most say Senegal.

In my own country, I am no longer recognised.

We become friends as time rolls on, almost as if auditioning today doesn't matter at all. I listen to their frustrated stories about the industry. A lot of them have been auditioning for years and never landed a role. I wonder why they're still returning and whether I would be half that patient. It seems that the industry isn't as easy as I pictured it.

My audition was an instant failure because I struggled to speak Pidgin English, my mother dialect. As I wait for an Uber to arrive, it occurs to me that, even now, I have a lot of hurdles to cross to make it in the industry. I have become a stranger in my own land and to my own people. I am feeling fragile and teary, knowing that I have nowhere else to run to. Returning to Nigeria to become a star was all I had dreamed of in Australia. Now, the country that I used to know has turned its back on me. I think that everything has betrayed me at this point, including my motherland.

One of the girls from the audition calls out to me, saying that Uber is a waste of money. She and her crew catch the bus and she suggest I join them. I don't know my way around, so I feel safer with Uber. Besides, I think that the buses are ten times worse that the cabs I was complaining about, and I am new here.

Chapter 11: Home

In Nigeria, passion was redefined for me. Nigerians work for their passion with whatever is available, no excuses. When I tell them all about the resources that I have back home in Australia – the resources they desire – they remind me that I have it all. People wonder what I am doing in Nigeria, what stopped me from reaching my dreams, asking the same questions that were posed to me by Emmanuel. Now I have the answer. I was the only person stopping me, and I know now that if I cannot make this dream work in Australia, I can never make it work anywhere.

The people are persistent and resilient here. I have become stronger, tougher and smarter too. I am no longer catching Ubers, and I have made some good friends.

I have been fortunate to feature in some projects. Other people have been auditioning for ten years with no luck, but I am getting noticed. Auditions become a catch-up for us all, and some of them are becoming jealous. They would say things like, 'I am going to stop going to auditions with Jessica. Jessica steals people's lucky stars." It was said with a smiling face, but I knew that the meaning was deadly serious.

OD – my best friend – added, 'If you get into a room with Jessica, her presence would grab all the attention so that no-one notices you and you are left in the dark.' Even though I tried not to pay much attention to what was being said, I knew they were right.

One day, I wanted to check out one of the local markets where they sell fine secondhand clothes. As OD and I were cruising around, every head would turn and some would stare. On our way out of the market, we bumped into some primary school kids. They started staring at me. At first it was one, and then two, and then three, four, five and now I'm crowded with their eyes and bodies, all begging to take pictures with me and asking whether I am a star. OD gets pushed aside until I can no longer see him in the crowd which is crushing me.

OD didn't have a good phone, so he would borrow mine to record stories. When he did this, I would remember my two high-end cameras that are back in Australia. OD hasn't got a laptop to write scripts with, yet he writes. I have three laptops, two of which are doing nothing back in Australia. He cannot afford editing software, yet he edits. Meanwhile, I have an annual subscription to the same editing software they use in Hollywood, but I hardly use it.

I know now why I came. My return to Nigeria wasn't to become a star, as I initially thought. It was to learn and re-learn. Nigerians are tough. They can make anything out of nothing and they do not allow their limitations to stop them. I had been crying and whinging about Nigeria, about how hard it is, regretting ever thinking this was going to result in something good… all the while, I was drinking in the strength, the resilience, the strategy and the thick skin of my people that I need to be able to tackle Australia.

I became a silent observer: observing the people, observing the world, observing myself. Now I cannot wait to return to Australia. This was what I needed, to re-taste the other side so that I could understand the value that is available elsewhere. I also needed to be reminded of who I am. I am a pure-born Nigerian. In my country, we make things happen wherever we find ourselves. How could I have forgotten that? *We make things happen* – that is the sound of Nigerian blood.

I left Nigeria knowing that I might never return again, at least not anytime soon. But I also know that it has given me the most valuable thing, and that is the spirit of my people's resilience, which I need to adapt to where I have found myself living. I returned to Australia as a different person. By the time the plane landed in Perth, I already knew that I wouldn't be backing down this time.

Either Australia would crush me, or would I crush Australia. Australia and I are going to roar against each other until one of us backs down and it isn't going to be me. I have been cooked, roasted and fried, and I am ready.

Chapter 12: Cumar

I can't afford rent, so Lucas lets me stay at our house with the children until I am able to move out again. I don't know how long that might take because I have a degree in filmmaking, where there are no jobs. What a joke. But I'm here for now, and I realise that I'm lucky. I don't pay for food either, Lucas sorts all that out. It's the perfect opportunity to give my dream a final try. Mind you, we are still fighting. The children are becoming used to it. Lucas never goes off at them, just me and his parents who live a few minutes' drive from here. We're his punching bags.

What is most disturbing is that Lucas will explode with anger over dinner, then wake up the next morning as if he doesn't remember what he did last night. He makes me nice coffees and asks how I slept. This has become the norm. We no longer look forward to enjoying dinner because we never succeed at it – somebody must smash a plate for the mistakes that have been made each day.

My first Sunday back in Australia was spent at the African Church I had discovered before travelling to Nigeria. One day, I was at uni when an African guy walked up to me and introduced himself as a fellow Nigerian. From there, he introduced me to his Church. I was shocked to learn that Australia has so many Africans living in White suburbs. I had been studying a course that seemed to be meant for White people, so I hardly saw any Black African people in Australia before this. Couple that with the fact that they serve Nigerian food after the service, and my butt becomes glued to those church pews.

Over time, the congregation and Pastor Daniel got to learn about me and my passion. Pastor Daniel understood the image of

Black people here in Australia and their lack of representation in the media. He was very impressed at my boldness, and every time he saw me, we would talk about it. He would constantly push me to go forward. 'Don't be afraid to knock at doors. Tell people your dream and what you want to do, I'm sure God will speak to them and they'll open that door for you'. He's got two growing daughters who could be dreaming of something other than nursing, and I feel that he is talking to me the way he would speak with them. Pastor Daniel always seemed like my biggest fan, so I am really happy to see him again.

That Sunday, Pastor Daniel prayed for me. I met a new member who ended up giving me a lift home and a phone number. He said, 'Speak to Tony, he'll hook you up.' I dialled Tony as I walked inside the house. As soon as I mention the word *media* to Tony – boom! – Cumar's phone number is sent to my phone. 'He is the best person I can direct you to,' he says.

Then I dial Cumar. Straight away, we connect – cutting words off and completing each other's sentences. He's talking, I am talking, you would think we knew each other already. He fills me in with all the things he's up to while I'm informing him of where I'm coming from and where I'm going. It was a long and exciting chat.

I met with Cumar one rainy day, and I was frustrated because he left me outside his center for an hour while it rained. When he finally opened the door, the puzzle pieces came together and I was reminded that nobody comes into your life by accident.

From the moment I met Cumar, my story changed. Through his eyes, I see not just my capabilities but also the possibilities and opportunities; I see the problems that linger in the African community here, the same problem I have seen right from beginning. Cumar knows what those problems are – he carries them as a constant weight across his shoulders.

I see the need for a change. I see revolution, a Black revolution. I have had enough, so have my people. The storyteller in me roars with hunger. The Nigerian blood in me screams!! I know who I am now. I'm a Nigerian, we make things happen. We create change.

We are the leaders of entertainment in Africa, and that is not by accident. I am a daughter of the same soil.

This is who we are.

The words *failure* and *fear* become silent in my ears. I roam the streets, speaking all of the language that I have gathered. 'Where are my people?' I demand to know, just like when I arrived – except this time, I am ready to go deeper. I want to purge the truths that surround them. The storyteller spirit in me is ready to write. I want to cast it all into the open for everyone to see. I spit my words out, smashing them on everyone's faces – call me a chatterbox if you want, I'll take it.

As I gather information about my people, I'm also gathering together the few of us that have had something to do with cameras. Our stories are similar, so they got the memo even before I even had the chance to ask if they would join with me.

It is time, I am ready to choose courage.

Stories start to come together, take shape and make meaning. The fact that most of my people tell the same stories about being forced into becoming someone they are not just to survive in Australia pained me the most, even though I already knew it. They confirmed what I saw in their faces from beginning – this is oppression! This is wrong!

I am pissed. Pissed at things that I can't put together. Pissed at my failed marriage. Pissed at the system. Pissed at myself, pissed at my people. I say *they* to describe who I am pissed at, and when I'm asked, 'Who are *they*?' I go blank. I really don't know or care at this point. My people must be free. Everyone should be allowed to do what they want to do. My blood boils. My colour shouldn't define my path. This has to stop. The fact that other people of colour have similar stories makes me boil even more. But it also clarifies to me who to point fingers at.

It ends here.

Chapter 13: Not So Scary

I tell Cumar that I want to make a TV show. He says he's got a story that he's working on for theatre and he's wondering whether we could turn it into a series. Cumar said we should speak to Screen Perth about the Western Australian government investing in our idea. I have learned to recognize opportunities when I see them, so I did not think twice about doing this.

It was as if the blinding fear had been ripped off my eyes. My presentation skills kicked in. My passion, raw and real, had been validated along the way and it had matured. Now it was clearer and fearless.

'Our stories need to be told!' I exclaim to Zoe, who was working with the Screen Perth Diversity and Inclusion Fund. She watches me, speechless, as if hearing this story for the first time. In my mind, there was no question what must happen.

'Put your application in,' she says as I walk out the door.

I never thought that someone like me could ever receive government funding. I always thought it would go to others - the smarty-pants and the White faces. Not people like myself, who come from a remote village in Nigeria. But less than two months later, I have it.

While everyone else thinks that 2020 is their worst year because of the Covid-19 pandemic, it has proven to be my best year so far. I have learned that the funding is to pay me and a mentor for time to spend together on this project. I'm excited about this funding – it is the first time I am earning since I moved to Australia and it's coming from something that I am passionate about, something that

I never thought was possible for a person like myself. That is incredible to me.

Everything became about writing for me. Lucas looked after the kids and all I did was write. He was happy for me and supported me however he could. He would still flip out sometimes, but no more than what had become usual. It was as if God knew that I needed a safe space to be able to create the stories and He gave me that safe space. I could tell from this point that I wasn't alone in my journey. I could feel an extra force navigating me all the way. It started to sink in that my life story had been written and I am just a character in it. The heat had come when it was necessary to drive me forward and toughen me up for the next level, and then it cooled off when I needed to reflect or to apply the strength that I had newly acquired.

The development of this series is more difficult than I anticipated. We are two months down the track and I am not making any progress. I am yet to produce even one character bio for *The Family*. In fact, it looks like I no longer know what the story is about, which is strange because it is the same story that was approved for the funding – so why is my mentor saying that the approved story no longer counts? This is getting me frustrated, since I am the writer. I should be in charge of what goes in and out. It appears that writers don't always know what is going to happen. It is the story that walks the writer through as they go, rather than the writer deciding which paths to take.

My mentor, Emily, is White. I am wondering if there is some foul play here. What else would explain the fact that she makes me repeat tasks over and over, yet she is still not satisfied? In a bid to smash through the barriers and move onto the next stage with *The Family*, I keep coming up with different themes, cramming them all together and hoping that my mentor will like something and sign off on going to the next stage. It seems that this is making things worse; whenever I'm pitching, she's staring at me from the other side of the table and giving me a look that makes me want to stop and say that I have had enough.

One day she stops looking at me that way. She speaks in a very gentle and calm tone. 'I think there's another story inside this story that you're trying to tell. Tell me more about this other story.'

Emily is right. My experience over the past ten years has filled me up with an overflowing pack of stories. I desperately want to fit them all in. What I did not realise was that a story works best when it focuses on one theme and explores it to the fullest.

'For your next task,' Emily concluded, 'I want you to put down everything you know about this other story of yours. Give it a title and we can talk about it when next we meet.' I shut down my laptop.

While pondering Emily's words, I wonder if this new story will distract me from *The Family*, which I was funded for. What if I don't complete the task before it is time to submit the outcome? Lots of worries start to kick in because I am already halfway through the scheduled six months. I don't know if I can produce a story bible and a pilot episode script by the end of this six months when I hardly know what the story is by now. In spite of all this, I am still trusting Emily. She's got a lot of experience.

Emily always tells me to not rush. 'Sit with it and it'll come. Go for a walk at the park. Don't force it, and the story you are meant to tell will come to you.' It sounds like some voodoo shit to me. Go for a walk? How can I be calm enough to go for a walk when I have a task ahead of me? I nod when she tells me to do it, knowing full well that I am not going to. I prefer to fight with my tasks until I get them finished. I am the one writing the story, I am not going to have the story writing me.

This other story did not waste a minute. It found its way straight into my head and out to my laptop. She tells me everything about her, this other story. She tells me how important she is, and how urgently she needs to be told. Not only that, she tells me what she should be called. *I'm Not a Nurse*. Her colour palette was shown to me, her tone and style – everything was in front of me, and then I have tears in my eyes.

This is me. For the first time, I am able to reflect on my journey over the past ten years in Australia and it is not a joke. While I was struggling in my journey and pushing for my passion, I was creating this story and bringing together pieces of the puzzle that makes up who I am, yet I did not know it. In this moment, I have broken my yoke. I am healed, and I am grateful.

I return to Emily with *I'm Not a Nurse*. She likes the story. For the first time, I am speaking fluently to Emily. I now see that she's not here to look down on me or make me feel inferior. She is really here to help and nurture me. Our struggles in the beginning have been from misunderstandings. Suddenly, all of the walls that existed between us vanish, and I am now looking at the woman who has been sent here to assist me. I now see what she meant by trusting your gut and that writing shouldn't stress you. The story that I have been carrying inside of me for years just wrote itself.

'*I'm Not a Nurse*. I like the title.' Emily smiles. She tells me the story is clear, focused, and relatable even though she's never walked in the shoes of people of colour like myself. Emily sees the importance of this story, that it is authentic and organic. 'I think you are ready to apply for Screen Perth's Elevate Fund.'

My heart flips in fear. A grant for emerging filmmakers in Western Australia that means I would be competing against the almighty smarty-pants White people? Does Emily think that I can compete against White people? What do I know? What story do I have that could outshine that of a White person? I might have won my first round of funding, but that was a diversity funding grant – White people weren't included. I'm not going to be up against them, I know I won't get it.

All that excitement from the new story is starting to shrink. I may as well just focus on the little money that I have been given, finish with it and move on to who knows what, maybe nursing or cleaning or whatever else there is that accepts migrant people of colour like myself and that doesn't have to put me in a fight against White people like the film industry. So long as I last in the film industry, this battle is never going to end. In my mind, I quit. Once this project that I'm working on is complete, that will be it between me and film.

The more I tried to focus on *The Family*, the more *I'm Not a Nurse* wants to be told. It is as if the earlier blockages I faced with *The Family* have now doubled, leaving me even more messed up and lost. This new story says that unless I complete it, nothing else happens.

Within weeks, I have scratched out the draft for this story and I am starting to have conversations with the different producers Emily has introduced to me. I like Sarah – she is funny and chatty and most of all, she is a Gemini like me. The first day Sarah and I met, which was on Zoom (due to a Covid-19 lockdown), we chatted for so long that it was as if we'd known each other for years. It was easy to bring Sarah into the world of my story. We agreed to get onto an Elevate grant application.

Sarah is so proud of my pitch video for the application. She told me that when she watched it, she felt compelled to share it with her mum. She said, 'Look at this incredible woman I am working with.' I feel satisfied that I have said everything I need to say in the pitch video. I cry every single time I watch it because the wounds feel fresh – my struggles that I have been through in Australia, in trying to belong and follow my passion. Watching the video takes me back to all of it, but it also reminds me of the fact that I am not alone, that my people are still living this struggle, and then I feel the roar boiling up inside me again. My people should be able to feel free to pursue what they are passionate about, not what is forced on them based on the colour of their skin.

This story has told me to have faith. I have trusted Emily, and now Sarah from beginning of this story. Emily is crossing her fingers for us to get the funding. We feel confident.

Now that *I'm Not a Nurse* is out of the way, I can focus on *The Family*. To my surprise, it is now starting to flow. I know what the story is about. My time with Emily becomes something I look forward to, and every single week seems to complete a marathon of progress. Emily has told me that I can ask for an extension of time. There was no point in panicking after all.

Everyone is proud of me. Lucas, and his parents – they are all proud of me. Lucas is not surprised. He is so confident that I will one day develop into the powerful woman that I am here to become. I am the only one shocked. Lucas is surprised that I am shocked. He puts me on the level of Michelle Obama and Oprah. He always has.

Chapter 14: When It Rains

I am shocked beyond words. Two grants awarded in a year? All the stories that I've always thought I'd never be able to tell, and Screen Perth picked *I'm Not a Nurse*. All of a sudden, I'm a very busy girl!

My face is circulated to the inbox of every filmmaker in Australia through Screen Perth funding announcement. The lecturers at UWA that I had lost touch with start emailing me and congratulating me. I was still in contact with one of them, Harper, who is a very good cinematographer. I have him in mind for filming this story, although Sarah has ideas about someone else. I listen to Sarah in all things, but this something I am adamant about.

During my first year at Uni, I saw Harper in a dream, telling stories with me. I didn't even know Harper very well. I remembered sharing that dream with Simon and laughing at it because I planned to move back to Nigeria, so I did not see it as a possibility. But Simon said to me, 'You never know.'

Things are moving very fast, and a lot is happening for me at the moment. I grab at opportunities to create a path for myself away from nursing. My understanding of the struggles that migrant people of colour face has lead Cumar and I to creating Sona Images – a platform that is to represent the stories of migrant people of colour and promote their talents. I see the need to drive our colourful stories into the Australian screen sector, to represent Australia for what it truly is. Cumar is on the same page. He is dark, tall and baldheaded, and he has a sense of humor that leaves me cracking up long after he has cracked his jokes. He draws attention and makes people want to keep listening to him, and he is as passionate about stories as I am.

While working to create Sona Images, another idea kicked in: *Black and Bold* magazine. Although my first challenge in Australia was the lack of people who looked like me on Australian screens, I later discovered a lack of confidence to be my other challenge. I was adoring, worshipping, fearing and feeling threatened by White people. I saw them as superior to me, and that wasn't just because of what they have in their brains; I was threatened by their beauty. I meet White people and I no longer see myself as beautiful. I trapped myself in a wig just so I felt like I could belong, or come as close as I can possibly could to belonging. I wore an Afro wig for a very long time to get attention, and that got me through surviving the loneliness of my time at university. That drew a few friends, so I thought that it worked. They assumed that the wig was my natural hair and I went with it to conceal my shame and what I saw as my ugliness. But how long was I going to remain trapped in wigs and lies?

When I finally broke free, I saw a shift in myself. I went from a woman who couldn't confidently speak to a White person to speaking with a group of them, pitching my ideas and captivating them with my passion like I used to back in Nigeria, doing it all with my bald head, with no makeup on, with my accent and my Black skin and I was not sorry for any of it. Now know who I am: a powerful Black woman embracing myself for who I am. At the bottom of this, I found the need to rediscover Black beauty, the goddess in us that we have left buried under the shadow of White wings in a bid to belong.

By the time I arrived at what I am going to do with *Black and Bold*, I found Jack, a designer. Although I went to him to seek his services in designing *Black and Bold* magazine, Jack wants to be an equal part of it. He adores the concept and he gets it. According to him, he is White but he has always had the passion to help uplift Black people. It feels right to let him in – he seems to have a lot of skills and experience. He is very good with details and the ideas he has dumped on the table for *Black and Bold* are taking the concept to another level. I was planning to keep it in Australia but we are now talking about going global.

Before I met Jack, I dreamed that I was going to create a mud house with no structure. And then a guy came to add structure and a proper foundation. I didn't know what that dream meant when I woke up, but after meeting Jack, I believe that he is that guy.

My home with Lucas and the children is peaceful at the moment, and I am hoping that very soon I can earn enough money to be able to rent a house and move out of this one. I apply for a scholarship to complete Curtin's Ignition training program so that I can create a talk show. *The Jessica Bailey Lounge* will bring together the media industry and migrant people of colour to address the issue of exclusion. It is place where I can share my experiences and hear from others who want to lead change towards a better and more inclusive Australia. My application is approved.

I complete the intensive training and I am ready to take over the world. Curtin's Ignition training taught me so much. The one week intensive course made me realise that only passion can drive you to cross all hurdles. When I realised how much work I needed to put into Ignition, I thought I wasn't going to survive it. Day one was already feeling like it was twelve years long, and when I finished, my eyes were heavy and my brain was packed and ready to explode. But with passion, I powered on and by the time I got to the end of the week, I didn't want Ignition to finish. It was packed with networks I never knew I could have in Australia. I met with Olivia Humphrey, who had a coffee with me. It was incredible, sitting with such an incredible entrepreneur in the media industry and chatting about my story. My good luck shined throughout the week and words were pouring down from my mouth like rain the entire time. Because I was the only African in the crowd as well as the only one in media, I was easily remembered. I start to realise that being different can sometimes work in our favour and I milked it.

Less than a week after I finish the Ignition program, Jack and I were halfway through creating the photo content for a *Black and Bold* coffee table book when he suddenly says that he doesn't want to continue with the business. His wife has given him an ultimatum. She has witnessed Jack painting the naked body of one of our models and she has seen me wearing Jack's jumper. She has told Jack to quit, or his family quits on him. The poor guy chose to do what's best for his family, sticking by them and quitting a business that is one year down the track and has swallowed all of my time and money.

I wailed a little when I shared this with Lucas, and he urged me to move forward. He truly knows how I feel inside. He gives me the warmest hug ever and looks at my face saying, 'I'm here for you. Whatever you need, I'll support you. You are a strong woman and you are on your way, so toughen up. I know you can do this. Don't think this is the end.'

I feel safe knowing that I've got his support and to me, it is like a parent's support; only parents can give you that deep sense of assurance. Hearing it from Lucas, I feel empowered again, as if I can count on him. The world is my oyster.

It's hard to nurture this baby on my own. It was great having someone like Jack to share the workload of *Black and Bold*, but oh well. As Lucas said, I've got everything it takes to do it.

Suddenly Lucas disappears. This man that has just given me his word has left me and the children with nothing more said. And just like Jack, it wasn't within his power to change course. He was taken away from me in the same week, and he is not coming back any time soon.

I have never been a mother. For the past ten years, Lucas has been playing the role of mother and father to our children. I never really felt like a mother. Maybe because I had them both through C-section and had never really known labour pain. Maybe because my boobs had never produced milk. Maybe because I am just not a mother and don't have motherhood in me. I don't have answers. How am I supposed to manage these children, a big house, and all of my projects by myself?

Lucas has been more of a parent to me than a husband since I arrived in Australia. He dealt with bills and all that it took to run the house. I drive a car but I have never been to a petrol station. Lucas solved all of those problems before I even knew they existed. I cannot manage myself, let alone the children and a household. But it doesn't look like I have a choice unless I return to Nigeria with my children – but that wouldn't be the best idea.

My life has just started, but the kids are calling on me because the internet has gone off, or a game requires a password that I have never known. School starts back next week and I am supposed to start getting them ready but I have no idea how. *I'm Not a Nurse* is in the middle of pre-production and I need to be scouting locations and completing vision boards. I canceled my next appointment with Sarah. I am fucked.

This can't be a coincidence. I wail and wail. Then my phone rings – it's Sarah. I am relieved to have someone to cry to.

'Jess…' Her voice shakes on the other end of the phone.

'Sarah, what is it? Are you okay?' Now I am panicking.

'I am so sorry that I have to do this.' She bursts into tears. I'm freaking out so badly that I start to hear my own heartbeats. 'Sarah, speak,' I plead.

'I know you are a strong woman Jess, I've always believed in you, ever since we met, and you inspire me a lot.' She tells me that she needs to step away from *I'm Not a Nurse*. We are both crying, we cannot control it. She says, 'When it rains, it pours, Jess,' and it feels like my heart leaves my body.

Who in the world did I offend? What and where did I go wrong? A week ago, things were in the perfect place; I had my short film funded, I had *Black and Bold* rolling on, I had Lucas looking after the children. I had it all, smashing my dreams with no apologies, just as it should be. Where did I make a mistake?

I take a walk around the house that Lucas has left me in; the three living rooms, bathrooms, kitchen, all the bedrooms. I look at my children and the completely uncontrollable situation before me and suddenly I burst into laughter. There's a way the universe deals with you, and you know for certain that's what is happening. I have been on my journey the whole time, but in this moment, my journey has just begun. I know it, my bones know it, everything in me knows it.

While working with Jack, he introduced me to two books; *The Game of Life and How to Play It* by Florence Scovel Shinn, and *Think and Grow Rich* by Napoleon Hill. Looking back, it's as if these books were why I met Jack. It shifted my perception about life and suddenly everything seemed to be possible. I started to understand the subconscious and conscious mind, and how we are responsible for everything that happens to us. Napoleon and Florence presented me with a way to ask for what I wanted. I wrote it all down without thinking about how I am going to acquire it. I would make it my prayer every night before I go to sleep, and having a peaceful house was on my list. With my filmmaking degree, I saw no possible way to acquire my own house and so I practiced calling it forth.

Now I have a six-bedroom house to myself and my children, and there's peace in my home. This is what I have prayed for. We stuff things up sometimes, but my kids and I laugh over it and my 5-year-old will go, 'Silly mummy,' and we'll laugh again. We have never been happier. I am not perfect, and I am not afraid to let them know that. I cry sometimes, then I'll wipe my tears. The strength in me swells.

Sona Images is still very promising. Cumar and I fight, but we settle with ease. Also, thanks to Jack leaving, the heart of *Black and Bold* magazine has shifted to what it originally was. I have realised that *Black and Bold* is a very personal brand, based on my lived experiences with beauty and confidence, and only I can sell it. I have also discovered that I can covert a space in my house into a home studio for *The Jessica Bailey Lounge*.

I'm Not a Nurse has attracted more interest than I ever anticipated. People are as hungry as I am to see this story come to life. Harper heard that we would need a new producer and said to me, 'I think Leo might be willing to come in on this project.' Since then, the story has skyrocketed. Leo, my former academic chair at UWA, has pulled everything together with his network: sound design, PA, you name it. Locations were sorted without breaking a sweat. All of the legal stuff for Screen Perth has been dealt with, and in a blink of any eye we have got a film in the can. It doesn't get any better than that.

I am no longer afraid of anything. If I don't know something, I find a way to learn it.

It feels like Heaven.

Afterword: Purpose

I know for sure that discrimination is real, whether conscious or unconscious, and so is racism. I have experienced it a few times, but I know people who have dealt with more and are still dealing with racism and discrimination in Australia. A friend shared with me how he almost changed his name because he gets pulled aside at the airport every single time he's travelling – even his UK citizenship does not protect him. Black people say to me, 'Jessica Bailey, you're so White with that name, people would give you a pass before they even meet you.' I used to feel like I should apologise for the name given to me. Now I have reached the point where I no longer feel sorry for who I am, and I suggest others do the same.

All of my wins and breakthroughs had compelled me to think that the system isn't what I first thought, and that it is we Black Africans who are guilty and responsible for what happens to us, and that we need to participate more in Australia. This started to swell my head so that I saw myself as a hero, and I would preach these messages to people without caring to hear their side of the story. I would say, 'Fear is what is tying our people down. We have laid blame on the system for years, but the system has been receptive all along. The system is free.' I spoke with confidence because I had lived it, and you couldn't tell me otherwise. I would say this in front of White people, and I would sense betrayal from the eyes of my fellow Blacks. Sometimes even White people were puzzled by my stance, and I could imagine them wondering what kind of person was sponsoring me in Australia, because I was not laying low or taking crappy jobs and that seemed to confuse them.

When I eventually got sick of listening to myself and started listening to other people, I saw where the misunderstanding was. I had been privileged. Being married to a middle-class white family protected me against the struggles that many Black African migrants go through in Australia. It made me oblivious to the stories of settlement and struggle and how survival is their daily meal. Many African migrants see coming to Australia as a privilege, so they put all their efforts into surviving and sending money back to the families they've left behind. This money would come from their own pocket, and they had sweated for it.

I was privileged beyond measure. I never asked to come to Australia, and my permanent residency was approved before I realized that it had been applied for. Unlike me, many Black African migrants pay rent, water bills and light bills, and they have no one to run to for rescue. I was oblivious to all of this, living in a mansion that belongs to my rich husband who comes from a family that owns many buildings. My mother-in-law's debit card lives in my wallet for emergencies, and I have an additional father figure who would chase mosquitos away before I notice their presence.

Now I see clearly. My people are not to be blamed for what they face. I see that I can no longer run from these problems because I am part of their solution. My children are the future of this nation and I am calling for urgent improvements in the representation of Black Africans in Australia. I have been privileged enough to crash through these obstacles which have left many buried. My dream of becoming a superstar no longer serves me – my dream has become to help my people see that they too can still meet their dreams, regardless of challenges. When I was given the privilege of creating my short film, *I'm Not a Nurse*, I chose to step back from acting so that more of my people could be involved with the story and make an impact. That made me happy – in fact, no happiness has equalled it. In the midst of trauma, I found my purpose.

Every person has a purpose in life. Unless you do that which you are called to do on this planet, no matter how much money you make, you can never completely be happy. There's always going to be that gap, that emptiness that keeps screaming for you to fill it.

Your purpose is what you're good at, it is what you'll eventually become an expert at and it is what gives you joy. Your passion is in your soul – you benefit from it even when you're not earning. You are to serve others through your purpose, and others are to serve with theirs. You are sitting on someone else's destiny when you are not moving with your own. The person your purpose would serve is not being served, and therefore would not receive what he or she is meant to have because you are not pursuing your goal.

I know for sure that fear controls us. I did not know about Screen Perth until my final year at university, and then I did not have the courage to approach them with my stories. Why? I was scared that nobody would want to have anything to do with my stories because of my heritage. When I finally met Screen Perth, it turned out I was wrong. I had exactly what they were looking for.

I want to inspire you. I want you to know that you are more than capable of your dreams and that you can become that person that you're born to become, no matter the obstacles and challenges that get thrown your way. I am telling this story to let you know that challenges will come – in fact, it is part of the process of becoming yourself. The bigger the goals, the bigger the challenge. Rather than letting it break you, let it make you. Let those challenges change you so that when you eventually come out the other side, you have a story to tell. I wouldn't be sharing my story if I hadn't learned that it's been all a process all along. Life is a puzzle, and it is the process of becoming that brings the pieces together.

I have come to realise that the challenges facing migrant people of colour in Australia should be treated as one of those challenges that face each of us with a goal. The more we realise and accept this, the more we can focus our energy on attacking those challenges rather than pointing fingers. We can play the victims for as long as we want but it won't solve anything.

I am certain that there are two voices influencing the career paths of people of colour in Australia. There's an unwritten code which, according to Collins Dictionary, is a rule, law or agreement that is 'understood and accepted by everyone, although it may not have been formally or officially established.' Urban Dictionary says it is a rule 'usually concerning social behavior which is known by all but spoken by none. This rule is neither official nor written down.' People of Colour (POC) such as myself feel pressured by others – that we only belong in certain sectors within the workforce. We are made to feel that we're not good enough, not worthy enough, we don't have the right qualifications or experience, or our cultural differences are too vast. This code is real, loud and merciless, and it decides for POC the path to follow, leaving us crippled with unhappiness.

The other voice comes from our homes – the families we've left behind. These voices are, to us, as powerful as the unwritten code. Many of us in the African diaspora are the breadwinners for our families – we put them first, which influences the path we follow. We sometimes make decisions based on other people's outcomes and experiences.

Many new culturally and linguistically diverse (CaLD) migrants hear stories about Australia from their community and assume that whatever value their community has already provided to Australia is the most that anyone from that community can contribute. They accept failure without even trying. This is a massive trap for skilled and talented migrants, who consign themselves and their families to offering less and gaining less from their new life in Australia.

We are better off trying and failing than not trying at all. My observation so far is that there is a misunderstanding between the CaLD community as well as the government agencies. Some government and industry representatives say they have to hunt for CaLD community members, whereas the CaLD people I speak to say they are unwanted. We must avoid living by assumptions. Opportunities are endless in Australia. Connect with people, especially if you're new to Australia. Don't be afraid to ask questions, find your community, and take your place.

The crazy thing about life is that the challenges don't stop unless you decide to stop growing. I might have overcome my initial challenges of not succumbing to the traditional narrative of Black migrants, but then came other challenges – my producer left right in the middle of pre-production for my short film. My business co-founder left before we launched the business. My husband suddenly left, abandoning me and all of our children.

I discovered that as I kept tackling challenges, it made me stronger. I have grown to know, love and cherish this beautiful country that I now call home. If we honour it, and work together to promote and grow Australia, that makes it ours. The future of Australia relies on us all working together in harmony. Data recorded by Worldometer shows the Australian population to be more than 25.7 million people in 2021. According to the Australian Bureau of Statistics (ABS), around one third of this figure were people born overseas, and almost half of the country had one or more of their parents born overseas.

The growth of every nation is directly reliant on its people. If the CaLD community occupies such a large percentage of the Australian population, it also means that a huge contribution is required from them for the nation to grow. While many CaLD communities are individually small, when classified by country of origin, Indian-born people are now the 3rd largest diaspora in Perth, after migrants of British and New Zealand origin.

The results of the 2016 national Census reveal that Australia is a fast changing, ever-expanding, culturally diverse nation. Australia is a multicultural, multireligious, and multiracial nation (as defined by Diversity Act Australia) and if this isn't reflected in industry key sectors, then businesses, industries and the economy suffer.

The screen industry, for example, talks about limitations in leadership without the input from important and diverse CaLD communities, and how this is affecting internal and external engagement locally, nationally, and internationally. In order for things to move forward in Australia, everybody must be adequately represented. If people's voices aren't being heard – their aspirations, ideas, concerns and problems – they cannot contribute effectively to the nation that they have chosen as their homeland.

Many come to Australia with dreams and passion, to better themselves, their families and the communities and nation in which we live. We come here only to get caught up in the tangle of an unwritten code, a code which effectively decides where people belong based on culture and skin colour, without asking questions about what skills, knowledge, international connections, and other resources or benefits have been brought to Australia with us. This code has swallowed and suppressed too many talents and potential leaders of Australia because they were not permitted to have a go at demonstrating how they could best contribute to growing Australia. I know this story not only because I have lived it, but because I have survived it.

For as long as we are not at creative, community, government and industry decision-making tables, the representation of the CaLD migrants to Australia will continue to be too low, and capitalising on the benefits of this migration will be too slow in coming.

What I've learned over the years is that only we can authentically represent ourselves. Over the years, I have cried and cast blame at White people who only wrote roles for White people in shows for White people to watch. Now I am writing my own stories – in the first one, my main character is Black; in the second, my main character is Black. When I wrote the third, I made it the same. It is time for communities to represent themselves.

Go represent you.

Acknowledgements

The stories in this book reflect the author's recollection of events. Some names, locations, and identifying characteristics have been changed to protect the privacy of those depicted. Dialogue has been re-created from memory.

BLACK&BOLD

www.ingramcontent.com/pod-product-compliance
Lightning Source LLC
Chambersburg PA
CBHW020328010526
44107CB00054B/2027